Witches

© Aladdin Books Ltd 1996

Designed and produced by
Aladdin Books Ltd
28 Percy Street
London W1P 0LD

First published in
the United States in 1996 by
Copper Beech Books,
an imprint of The Millbrook Press
2 Old New Milford Road
Brookfield, Connecticut 06804

Design
David West Children's Book Design
Designer
Flick Killerby
Editor
Jim Pipe
Picture Research
Brooks Krikler Research
Illustrators
Susanna Addario, Paola Holguín,
Lorenzo Pieri, Claudia Saraceni, Thomas Troyer –
McRae Books, Florence, Italy

Printed in Belgium

Library of Congress Cataloging-in-Publication Data

Ross, Stewart.
Witches / by Stewart Ross: illustrated by McRae Books Agency.
p. cm. -- (Fact or fiction)
Includes index.
Summary: The story of real-life witches through the ages.
ISBN 0-7613-0452-5 (lib. bdg.). --
ISBN 0-7613-0467-3 (pbk.)
1. Witchcraft--Juvenile literature. 2. Witchcraft--History--
Juvenile literature. [1. Witchcraft.] I. Title. II. Series: Ross,
Stewart. Fact or fiction.
BF1566.R65   1996
133.4'3--dc20   95-38885
                                              CIP   AC

FACT *or* FICTION:

Witches

Written by *Stewart Ross*
Illustrated by *McRae Books, Italy*

COPPER BEECH BOOKS
BROOKFIELD, CONNECTICUT

CONTENTS

INTRODUCTION

It's Halloween. Children put on frightening masks and costumes to go "trick or treating," a custom that dates back to the beginning of history. Is it harmless fun – or a sign of something more sinister?

Deep in everyone's mind lurks a fear of evil. It has always been there. All societies have their devils or evil spirits. And where there is wickedness, there are those who are said to worship it with rituals and magic. These are the witches, the ministers of mischief and sin.

But who is a witch? Few people willingly admit to practicing witchcraft, yet witches have always been found. Their foul deeds explain sickness and ruin, deformity and death. Over the centuries, thousands of witches have been persecuted and brutally murdered.

Did they deserve such gruesome fates? Did they actually ride on broomsticks and brew foul potions? Could they really summon up the devil? Or were they simply misunderstood misfits, the innocent victims of human ignorance and blind terror?

Welcome to the weird world of witchcraft! Close the curtains, pull up a chair by the fire, and read on. But first lock the door behind you. Just in case...

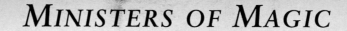

MINISTERS OF MAGIC

There are countless witch stories. Today, not many people really believe in witches and their powers (*left*), although they like to read about them in books or see them in scary films.

Not long ago, it was all very different. Magic and witches were taken seriously. When things went wrong, people looked for someone to blame. They singled out a lonely or misunderstood woman and said she was a witch with wicked powers from the devil or an evil spirit. Some just picked on people they didn't like.

These often innocent victims were frequently tortured to make them confess their wicked ways. Then they were killed, usually by being burned alive. Some men made a living just by catching witches!

WHATEVER WILL BE...

Will it rain tomorrow? Where is the treasure buried? Since the beginning of time, men and women have practiced sorcery, the art of revealing hidden matters using means other than the five senses.

There are many forms of sorcery: fortune-tellers gaze into crystal balls; numerologists believe in the power of numbers; palmists sees people's lives in the lines on the palms of their hands (*below*); astrologers read the future in the stars; and others use tarot cards (*right*), tea leaves – or even sandals tossed into the air! Science or superstition?

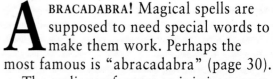

S	A	T	O	R
A	R	E	P	O
T	E	N	E	T
O	P	E	R	A
R	O	T	A	S

ABRACADABRA! Magical spells are supposed to need special words to make them work. Perhaps the most famous is "abracadabra" (page 30).

The earliest reference to it is in a poem of the second century A.D. Magic word squares, like the one on the *left*, were also popular with witches and sorcerers.

Wise Words

The words "witch" and "wizard" come from the Anglo-Saxon word wicca, *meaning wise one, as traditionally, witches were often linked with learning, especially medicine. No witch was complete without a book of spells and magic formulas, known as a* grimoire *(right).*

But the medieval church decided that all learning that did not come directly from God was the work of the devil. So knowledge of such secret formulas could get you burned alive!

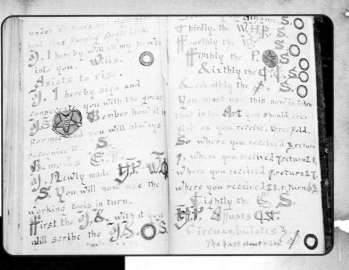

A TRADITIONAL WITCH *In the film* The Witches *(1989), based on a story by Roald Dahl, Angelica Huston (left) starred as a typically nasty witch who plans to turn the children of England into mice using a powerful magic potion.*

WITCH WAY FORWARD?

Witch doctors (*right*) are magicians that fight against evil spells and cure illnesses using traditional herbal remedies. In 1976, the World Health Organization (WHO) recommended that witch doctors should join African medical teams.

People don't visit witch doctors just because they believe in magic – often there is no one else to turn to when they are ill. Even today, modern medicines are just too expensive for many of the world's poor.

THE POWERS OF DARKNESS

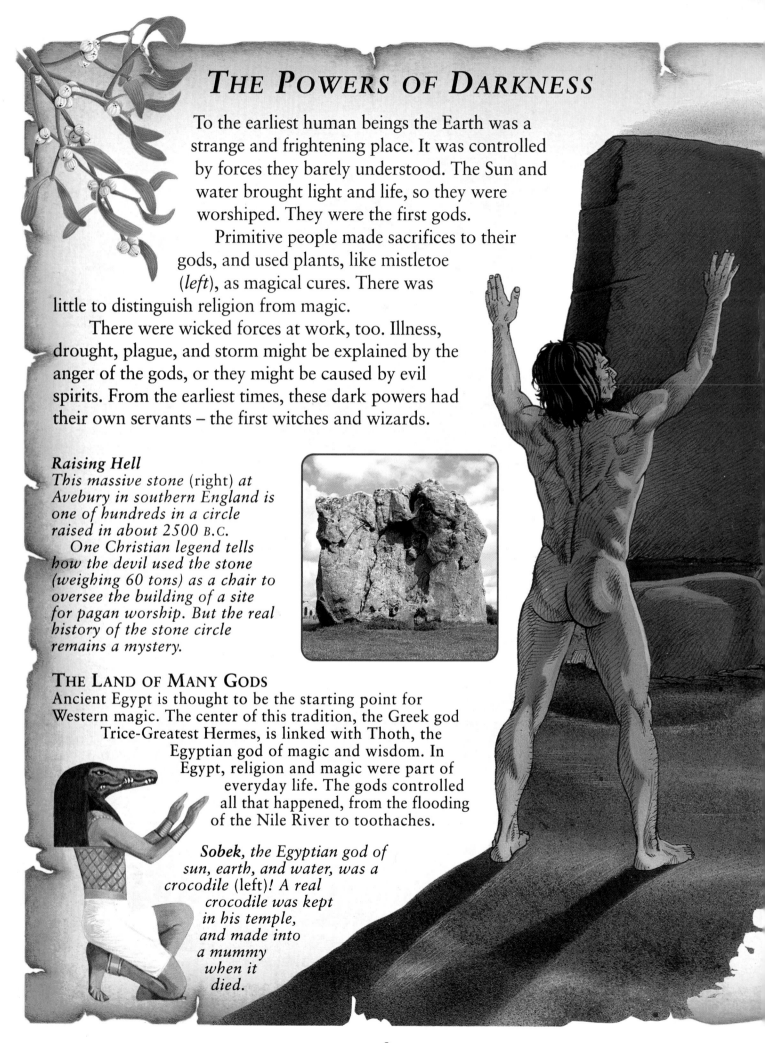

To the earliest human beings the Earth was a strange and frightening place. It was controlled by forces they barely understood. The Sun and water brought light and life, so they were worshiped. They were the first gods.

Primitive people made sacrifices to their gods, and used plants, like mistletoe (*left*), as magical cures. There was little to distinguish religion from magic.

There were wicked forces at work, too. Illness, drought, plague, and storm might be explained by the anger of the gods, or they might be caused by evil spirits. From the earliest times, these dark powers had their own servants – the first witches and wizards.

Raising Hell
This massive stone (right) at Avebury in southern England is one of hundreds in a circle raised in about 2500 B.C.

One Christian legend tells how the devil used the stone (weighing 60 tons) as a chair to oversee the building of a site for pagan worship. But the real history of the stone circle remains a mystery.

THE LAND OF MANY GODS
Ancient Egypt is thought to be the starting point for Western magic. The center of this tradition, the Greek god Trice-Greatest Hermes, is linked with Thoth, the Egyptian god of magic and wisdom. In Egypt, religion and magic were part of everyday life. The gods controlled all that happened, from the flooding of the Nile River to toothaches.

Sobek, the Egyptian god of sun, earth, and water, was a crocodile (left)! A real crocodile was kept in his temple, and made into a mummy when it died.

Mother Power

In early religions, beliefs and practices centered around basic issues, such as the growth of new crops each year and the birth of children.

The Earth itself was often seen as a mother figure (as shown in this carving, right) for without women, there could be no new life.

A MAN'S WORLD – AND HEAVEN

The modern religions, particularly Christianity and Islam, were founded by men. Their God was a man, too. Women were condemned as inferior to men and the source of wickedness.

The Bible story of Adam and Eve is a good example of this. In some ways, Eve was the first witch, tempting Adam to take a bite from the apple.

Mysteries of the Standing Stones

Western Europe is littered with the awe-inspiring and mysterious relics of prehistoric places of worship (main picture).

Sometimes great blocks of stone stand alone or in small groups. Elsewhere they are laid out in precise rows or circles, as at Stonehenge, in southern England.

These ancient sites are now a place of worship focus for modern druids.

THE FIRST SORCERER. Some of the finest prehistoric paintings are on the walls of limestone caves in southern France (*above*). In the Cave of the Three Brothers, a painting shows a dancing figure, half-man, half-beast, with the spreading horns of a stag.

Is this some ancient sorcerer or a vision of the Horned God worshiped by later pagan cultures? Other pictures of animals such as mammoths and deer are more than decoration, but we can only guess at their religious or magical meaning to our remote hunter ancestors.

THE GOLDEN ASS

The following story comes from *The Golden Ass,* a comedy written by the Roman Lucius Apuleius in the 2nd century A.D. The supposed powers and practices of witches described in his book hardly changed over the next 1,800 years.

A young student has run out of money. So, for a fee, he agrees to protect a dead body from scavenging witches. He has to remain alert, as they can turn themselves into any creature. During the night, he sees nothing but a little weasel, which he chases away. In the morning, the body looks intact. But its nose and ears are made of wax. A witch in the form of a weasel has stolen the real ones to use in her potion!

The Oracle at Delphi (top) *was famous for its cryptic prophecies. When King Croesus asked if he would defeat his enemy Cyrus, the prophetess replied merely that "A great empire will fall."*

Convinced he would win, Croesus launched an attack but was defeated by Cyrus. The angry Croesus returned to the oracle, only to be told it had meant that his empire would fall, not Cyrus's!

GODDESS OF THE UNDERWORLD

Hecate was a Greek goddess of the Underworld with great powers of sorcery (*above*). As late as the 11th century A.D., followers of her cult offered a food sacrifice (including black puppies and lambs) at the end of each month.

Lucius (main picture), *the sorcerer's apprentice in* The Golden Ass, *watches the witch Pamphile turn herself into a bird by smothering her body with magic ointment. Trying to copy her, he uses the wrong ointment and becomes a donkey!*

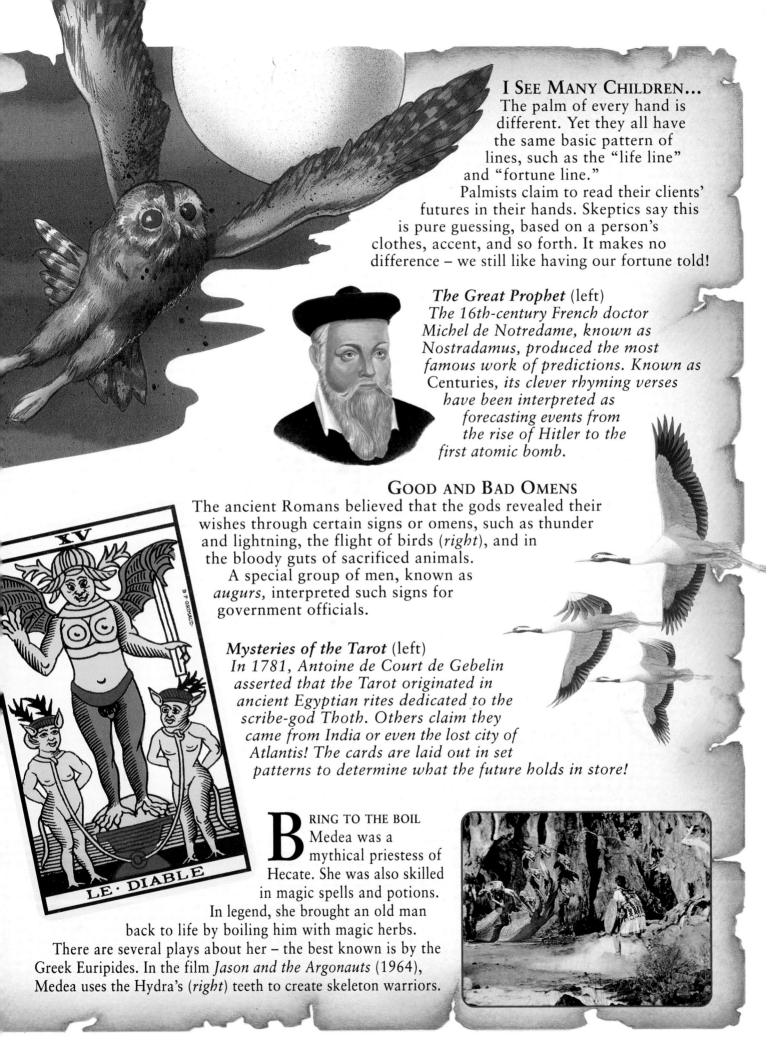

I SEE MANY CHILDREN...

The palm of every hand is different. Yet they all have the same basic pattern of lines, such as the "life line" and "fortune line."

Palmists claim to read their clients' futures in their hands. Skeptics say this is pure guessing, based on a person's clothes, accent, and so forth. It makes no difference – we still like having our fortune told!

The Great Prophet (left)
The 16th-century French doctor Michel de Notredame, known as Nostradamus, produced the most famous work of predictions. Known as Centuries, *its clever rhyming verses have been interpreted as forecasting events from the rise of Hitler to the first atomic bomb.*

GOOD AND BAD OMENS

The ancient Romans believed that the gods revealed their wishes through certain signs or omens, such as thunder and lightning, the flight of birds (*right*), and in the bloody guts of sacrificed animals.

A special group of men, known as *augurs,* interpreted such signs for government officials.

Mysteries of the Tarot (left)
In 1781, Antoine de Court de Gebelin asserted that the Tarot originated in ancient Egyptian rites dedicated to the scribe-god Thoth. Others claim they came from India or even the lost city of Atlantis! The cards are laid out in set patterns to determine what the future holds in store!

XV

LE · DIABLE

BRING TO THE BOIL
Medea was a mythical priestess of Hecate. She was also skilled in magic spells and potions.

In legend, she brought an old man back to life by boiling him with magic herbs.

There are several plays about her – the best known is by the Greek Euripides. In the film *Jason and the Argonauts* (1964), Medea uses the Hydra's (*right*) teeth to create skeleton warriors.

POPES AND PAGANS

As Christianity was spreading through Europe, missionaries tried not to upset people of other beliefs. They adapted existing customs rather than condemn them.

Pagan Europeans believed in witchcraft. The witch as an elderly, wrinkled hag – not the dangerous beauty of the classical world – came from Germanic culture. The early Christian leaders dared not persecute witchcraft, but suggested that Christianity was a superior belief. Later, when the Church's position was secure, it went on the attack and began the most vicious persecution of witches of all time.

CHILDREN OF WITCHES

The Huns, a nomadic people from central Asia (*left*), invaded Europe in the 4th century A.D. Because no one was sure where these tough and aggressive people came from, there was a popular myth that they were descended from witches!

Did King Arthur's Merlin Ever Exist? (main picture)
A singer from the 6th century A.D., called Myrddin, may also have been a seer. But the Merlin of legend was invented by Geoffrey of Monmouth in the 11th century, based on earlier Celtic myths. In these he lives only in the mind – a link between the living and the dead.

SINISTER SCRATCHES

The runic alphabet, or *futhark*, is the oldest writing from northern Europe. Used by the Vikings, its sinister-looking letters (*below*), found scratched on stones and pieces of wood, were said to be magical signs with mystical meanings. Try writing your name in this secret code!

A B C D E F G H I K L M

T HE NIGHT OF THE EVIL. Halloween (*left*) may have begun as a pagan festival adapted by the Christian church. According to legend, on one winter's night all witches and evil spirits came out of hiding. Today's "Trick or Treat" custom may have arisen from the wish to leave presents (treats) to keep them away.

The Church put the night of evil on the evening before Hallowmas or All Saints Day. This symbolised the saints' victory over the forces of the devil.

THE MAGIC OF THE CELTS

The Celts inhabited much of north-west Europe at the time of the Roman invasions. They had many gods and goddesses, such as the Green Man (*right*), a symbol of nature. Celtic mother goddesses are frequently shown carrying children or baskets of fruit – a far cry from the witches of the Christian era.

There were Celtic witches, too. Jealous Fuamnach, mythical queen of king Midir, turned her husband's second wife into a butterfly!

MISSIONARIES AND MAGIC

The Europeans of the pre-Christian era believed in wizards, witches and magic. So when the Christian missionaries appeared, they were expected to reveal magical powers to rival those of the old gods and goddesses. The miracles of the New Testament were interpreted as magic, and before long new miracles were proclaimed.

Snake in the Grass
One of the best stories was about St Patrick, the man who took the Christian faith to Ireland.
He is supposed to have shown the power of the new religion by ridding the country of snakes (left).

A MAGICAL BATTLE. Merlin (*above*), in the 1981 film *Excalibur*. The film highlights Merlin's battles against Morgan Le Fay, Arthur's half-sister and enemy. Morgan, who in legend could fly and lived with eight sisters on the isle of Avalon, may have been based on the Irish Morrigan, the crow goddess.

N O P Q R S T U/V/W X Y Z

SERVANTS OF THE DEVIL

In the center of a small town in southern France a young soldier stands chained to a stake. Around him lie piles of wood. Priests chant. Women weep. The signal is given and the executioner sets the wood on fire. Soon the condemned man is engulfed in flames.

Suddenly, there is a stirring in the crowd. A young girl pushes her way to the front and throws herself into the fire to perish alongside her lover (*main picture*). The victims were Cathars, a sect noted for their piety and charity. They were also unbelievers in the Church's eyes. The Church's attitude to wayward beliefs had changed.

The Devil (above) – *To medieval minds, the devil was a constant threat, waiting to pounce on human weakness.*

The Great Hunt
After Pope Innocent III condemned the Cathars in 1208, over 400 villages were destroyed in the hunt. Any Cathars refusing to recant were killed. Many fled to castles such as Peyrepertuse (left) near Roussillon.

THE TWO FACES OF GOD
The ancient gods were cruel and kind. How else, people asked, could evil exist?

The Christian God was an almighty and loving creator. But skeptics said that if God really was almighty, He must have created good and evil. Mani the Persian was crucified for saying this in 276 A.D. In the Middle Ages, Mani's ideas were adapted by the Cathars. To the Church such beliefs were heresy. It had to be eliminated.

FAIRY TALES. European fairy tales are full of witches and magic. A witch captures Hansel and Gretel and threatens to eat them – as witches were thought to dine on human flesh.

A witch uses her magic to help a couple have a baby daughter, Rapunzel. The witch takes Rapunzel, imprisons her in a tower (*right*), and visits her by climbing up the girl's long hair. Today such tales are read as children's stories. But when they were first told, they were terrifyingly real.

A magical symbol from Persia (above).

EASTERN MAGIC

From the 11th century onward, European Christians launched Crusades to recapture the Holy Land from the Muslims. This brought them into contact with Islam, the Muslim religion which accepted magic, and witches.

Picatrix, an Arab handbook of practical (known as "natural") magic, became popular in later medieval Europe.

MIDNIGHT HAGS

Three witches stand over a cauldron, chanting:

"Round about the cauldron go
In the poisoned entrails throw.
Toad, that under cold stone…
Boil thou first i' the charmed pot…
Eye of newt and toe of frog,
Wool of bat, and tongue of dog,
Adder's fork and blind-worm's sting…"

In the evil ingredients go, until the foul-smelling potion is ready.

The play is William Shakespeare's *Macbeth*. The witches are the "midnight **hags**" who have prophesied that Macbeth will be king.

No other drama in the English language captures so vividly the wicked powers and practices of witches.

A Traditional Witch
(right) *surrounded by cauldrons, charts, spell books, wands, broomsticks, candles, and potion bottles.*

MIRROR, MIRROR ON THE WALL Snow White's evil stepmother has many of the characteristics of a traditional witch.

She has a magic mirror (*above*), and uses disguises and a poisoned apple to try to kill her innocent stepdaughter.

Birds of Doom
A raven watches a witch cast her spell. These solitary birds (with feathers the color of night) were often associated with witchcraft.

SOUNDS FAMILIAR
Witches were said to have owned animals, known as familiars, to help them with their wicked magic. Cats and toads were given strange names like Little Tom Twit, Greedigut, and Pyewacket. Japanese witches used dogs, while those in Africa relied on owls (*top*) or baboons.

Black cats (right) *were the best-known familiars in Europe. Even today, some people are superstitious about them crossing their path.*

TUBBY TERRORS. Shakespeare, like many people of his time, was fascinated by witches and witchcraft. So was the Scottish king, James VI. This was why the playwright set *Macbeth* in Scotland and gave the witches such an important part in the story.
European witches were generally thought of as wrinkled and old. This image was not the same in other parts of the world, however. In Africa, for example, they were supposed to grow fat by feasting on human flesh!

THE WITCHES OF EASTWICK
Based on a book by John Updike, this story tells of three women (*above*) who, bored by life in a small town, discover they have magical powers.

17

THE WITCHES' HAMMER

Heinrich Kraemer and Jakob Sprenger, both learned Dominican priests, were convinced that Germany was being overrun by devil-worshiping witchcraft. They were determined to eliminate it.

In 1486, they produced a witch-hunter's handbook, known as *The Witches' Hammer*. One of the worst books ever written, it explained what witches were and how to recognize and capture them. Witches were shown as a well-organized sect plotting to overthrow God. The pope gave it his hearty approval and the book was soon in the hands of hundreds of would-be witch-hunters.

The book gave enormous power to popular beliefs that had previously been little more than superstition or spiteful gossip. In the madness that followed, perhaps as many as 300,000 "witches" were executed.

Supreme Power
Medieval popes (top) *were the supreme authority in the Christian Church. Their condemnation of witchcraft could not be challenged.*

FEASTING WITH THE DEVIL (*above*)
A Sabbat was a gathering of witches with the devil. The Inquisition first recorded a Sabbat in the 14th century. This took place in the Cathar region of southern France.

Before long, Sabbats were being described in confessions from witch trials all over Europe. However, there is no real evidence that these rituals ever took place (see also pages 40–41).

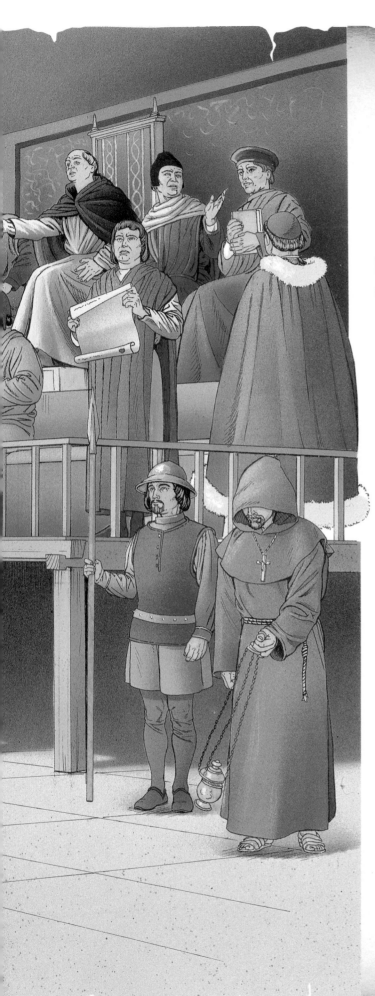

Know Thine Enemy! (main picture)
Founded by the Catholic Church in 1229 to eliminate heresy, the Inquisition led the attack on witches. At one time the Spanish Inquisition was reportedly burning 100 witches a day!

Inquisition trials were secret. The accused were not told who had denounced them and torture was widely used to obtain confessions.

SEALING THE WITCHES' FATE

Several papal bulls *(see below)* had already condemned sorcery and witchcraft. But the most effective was Pope Innocent VIII's *(left) Desiderantes Affectibus*, granted at the request of Kraemer and Sprenger in 1484.

The pair had met a lot of opposition, but the bull gave them power over the law courts and even bishops.

The Papal Bull
A pope's official pronouncements were made in the form of a papal bull. This was a document written in Latin, signed by the pope and sealed with a lead seal.

The word "bull" comes from bulla, *the Latin for a seal. A bull was known by its opening words.*

THE PRICE OF PLEASURE. The legend of Faust originated in medieval Germany and was turned into the play *Dr. Faustus* (1588) by the British playwright Christopher Marlowe.

Bored with science, Faustus *(right)* turns to magic. He summons up a servant of darkness and sells his soul to the devil. In return, he can have whatever he wants for 24 years. When his time is up, Faustus is led down to hell and eternal damnation.

"THANK GOD..."

A peasant asked his wife to take him to a witches' Sabbat. She agreed only when he had promised not to mention God's name.

The devil was present, and the man watched the dances and ceremonies with amazement. Then came the feast. The man asked for salt. "Thank God!" he exclaimed when it arrived. Immediately, the Sabbat vanished and the man found himself on the grass miles from home.

This tale of witch-hunting comes from a 16th-century Italian court, where the peasant told this version of events. On the basis of his words, his wife was found guilty of witchcraft and burned at the stake. Whether the peasant really believed what he said is unclear, especially given that many witnesses were tortured until they confessed.

Salty Superstitions
Salt (above) – *essential to human life – has always been a symbol of good. The superstitious say that spilling salt is unlucky.*
Friday, the day of the Sabbat, is also unlucky, especially Friday the 13th.

Flying Tonight
The belief in the witch's power to fly (above) *had existed long before the Greek witch Pamphile (page 10). Legends of flying witches abound, like that of the Nithsdale witches, who rode broomsticks decorated with dead men's bones.*
The besom *(broom) that we now associate with witches, was only rarely mentioned in 16th-century trials, though "not guilty, no flying" is a common entry in records.*

SIZE OF A NEWT!
Assisted by the power of the devil, witches were said to be able to do any number of magical things.

This included changing themselves into a living creature (favorites were owls, goats (*right*), and mice). This was done by rubbing their naked bodies with a special ointment.

Invisible arrows (left) *shot by witches at their victims were supposed to be the cause of ills from lameness to madness.*

EVIL DEEDS
The most common complaint against witches was that they caused harm to others. Sometimes this was done by poison. More often it involved charms or potions. By making models of the victims and sticking pins in them, witches could make them sick or even die.

Saved by the Salt (main picture)
The Sabbat disappears into thin air when a peasant mentions God. He had already aroused suspicion by asking for salt. Witches avoided salt, especially at Sabbats with the devil.

THE WITCHES' ARTIST. The great Spanish artist Francisco Goya (1746–1828) often made witches the subjects of his paintings. His early work suggests that he viewed witches as poor unfortunates who should be spared from persecution. Eighty etchings, known as the *Caprichos*, were reported to the Spanish Inquisition for undermining the teaching of the Church.

Goya's later witch paintings (*above*) are more sinister. Deaf and unhappy, he seemed to put his own dark fears of the unknown into his paintings.

"BURN THE LOT!"

Martin Luther (1483–1546), the founder of Protestantism, attacked many aspects of the Catholic Church. But not witchcraft.

Protestants followed closely the words of the Old Testament, which proclaimed, "Thou shalt not suffer a witch to live." Asked about witches, Luther said, "I would have no pity for them! I would burn the lot!"

THE WITCH-FINDER GENERAL

Matthew Hopkins (died 1647), the self-styled Witch-Finder General (*left*), made a living by terrorizing the English countryside as he traveled around looking for likely victims.

Hopkins bullied and tortured suspects and searched them for "devil's marks," such as warts or birthmarks. To Hopkins and his cruel cronies these were sure signs of devil worship.

Many innocent men and women died as a result of the witch-finder's accusations. He was so unpopular that when he died a rumor was started that he had failed his own swimming test (*main picture*) and been hanged as a witch!

SCOT'S SCORN

Despite the wave of persecution sweeping through Europe, by the reign of Elizabeth I (1558–1603) a number of Englishmen were questioning the existence of witchcraft. Reginald Scot, a member of parliament, expressed his doubts in *The Discoverie of Witchcraft* (1584).

The book criticizes witch hunters, and says that witches are simply innocent old people who are too poorly educated to defend themselves.

TRIAL BY WATER (*above*)

Hopkins' favorite test for witchcraft was "swimming." Although technically illegal since 1219, it had been given official approval by James I (page 23).

• The suspected witch was stripped and immobilized by tying her left thumb to her right big toe and her right thumb to her left big toe.
• A rope was tied around her waist, with one end held on either bank of a river. She was then pulled three times into the deepest water.
• If God allowed her to float (which could be faked by pulling on the ropes), she was a witch. If she sank, she was innocent. Not surprisingly, many drowned.

KINGS AND WITCHCRAFT

King James I of England (James VI of Scotland, *right*) was fascinated by witchcraft. When witches were accused of trying to sink a ship he was traveling in, he made a study of their practices. He wrote up the results in *Demonology*, which became a standard text on witchcraft.

King Henry III of France (left) was a seedy and warped character. However, the constant reports that he practiced devil-worship ultimately led to his assassination in 1589.

GET AGRIPPA!

Not only women were persecuted for witchcraft. Heinrich Cornelius Agrippa was a scholar with a reputation for practicing magic (his Great Magic Circle is *right*).

Denounced as a magician, he was pursued across Europe and eventually caught and tortured, dying in 1535.

KID'S STUFF

Children played a major role in the witchcraft mania. Witches were said to enjoy eating the soft flesh of the young. They were also accused of stealing babies so they could chop them up and use their parts in potions.

Children were also important to witch hunters. Terrified by what adults might do to them, they often gave false evidence in court. In 1527 two Spanish girls, aged 9 and 11, confessed to being witches and led the authorities to 150 others.

Out of the Fire and into the Noose
In England witches were hung, not burned (left). A witch-finder is getting paid on the far right of the picture.

Until the 18th century, there was little to separate science and magic in many people's minds. The friar Roger Bacon (1214–1294) was a philosopher, scientist, and mathematician. But he also spent hours and hours on alchemy. This was a search for the "elixir of life" (the secret of life) and a means of turning all metals into gold. It was rumored that Bacon once got the devil to help him bring a brass head to life!

The alchemist Albertus Magnus (1193–1280) was a bishop. He carried out many genuine chemistry experiments but was still thought of as a magician. In one story he brought a robot to life!

A WITCH TOO FAR

The German George Geiss was a fanatical witch-finder. But when he arrested the popular local miller and his wife, he had gone too far. The miller's friends banded together and lowered him from his cell on a rope (*above left*). Geiss was furious and burned the miller's wife. The enraged citizens beat up Geiss in the town square and reported him to the authorities.

Later, while chasing one of his victims, the cruel man fell from his horse and broke his neck. It was divine justice, his enemies said.

CHANGING FOR THE WORSE. A common accusation against witches was that they used evil powers ("glamor") to hypnotize people into seeing illusion as reality.

In many fairy tales ugly old hags suddenly turn into beautiful young girls (*above*), or a pumpkin is transformed into a marvelous coach (as in *Cinderella*).

The Indian rope trick, in which the fakir (magician) sends a boy up an imaginary rope, depends on the fakir convincing the audience to see what does not exist. Modern illusionists like David Copperfield also rely on such techniques.

The Secret Science
The alchemist at work in his laboratory. Alchemists were supposed to be pure in heart and mind, and their work was regarded as legitimate science.

Experiments were written down with a magical-looking symbol representing each chemical (see page border).

THE "COMPANION OF HELLHOUNDS"

Doctor John Dee (1527–1608, *right*), the explorer, and scientist, also dabbled in magic and claimed to have found the key to eternal life! This terrified his contemporaries, who knew him as the "companion of hellhounds."

In the reign of Mary I ("Bloody Mary," 1553–1558) Dee was accused of trying to kill the queen by using magic. Mary's sister, Elizabeth I, was more tolerant and made Doctor Dee her court mathematician.

THE SORCERER'S APPRENTICE

To save his village from ruin, a boy became an apprentice to a wicked sorcerer. In time he learned some of the sorcerer's secret spells and fought a magic battle with his master (*below*).

When the sorcerer became a bear, the boy became a snake. Finally, the sorcerer changed himself into a drop of water and was washed away!

GIFTS FOR THE DEVIL

It was extremely difficult for those accused of witchcraft to prove their innocence, as this story shows.

In 1646, several women from the Italian town of Castelnovo suffered miscarriages. An explanation was needed. The most obvious was witchcraft, and the old and ignorant Maria Salvatori was duly accused.

She was said to save the communion host as a present for her master, the devil (*main picture*).

Maria denied the charge. But under torture she confessed to being a witch and named other accomplices. The unfortunate Maria died in prison. Her supposed fellow witches were hanged and their bodies burned.

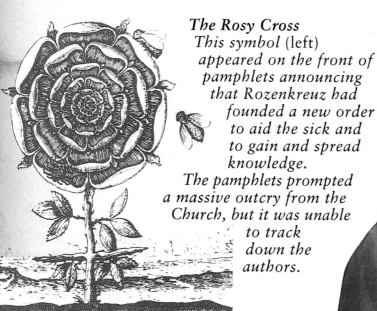

The Rosy Cross
This symbol (left) *appeared on the front of pamphlets announcing that Rozenkreuz had founded a new order to aid the sick and to gain and spread knowledge.*
The pamphlets prompted a massive outcry from the Church, but it was unable to track down the authors.

THE REBIRTH OF ALCHEMY

The language of alchemy was adopted by a group of 17th-century religious reformers known as *Rosicrucians*.

Followers of a mysterious writer known as Christian Rosenkreuz ("Rosy Cross"), they claimed secret magical powers that allowed them to turn base metals into gold, extend human life, and control evil spirits.

It's IN THE STARS. The age-old belief in astrology holds that the Sun, Moon, and stars affect everything that happens on Earth. Personality is determined by a person's "horoscope" – the position of heavenly bodies at their birth.

Although challenged by modern astronomy, astrology remains popular and millions still check their "stars" in the daily newspapers.

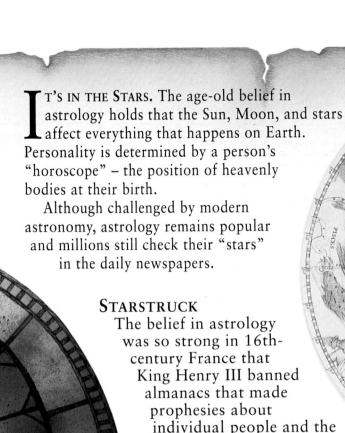

STARSTRUCK

The belief in astrology was so strong in 16th-century France that King Henry III banned almanacs that made prophesies about individual people and the kingdom. Had he not done so, he might have lived longer – he was murdered ten years later!

The Invisible College

In 1623, placards in Paris announced the existence of the Invisible College – a group of scientists who had renounced God in return for magical powers of flight and invisibility. Though probably just a joke, it inspired the creation of the Royal Society in London, one of the first scientific organizations in the world. Among its founders were Isaac Newton, chemist Robert Boyle, and physicist Robert Hooke.

Math and Magic

Sir Isaac Newton (1642–1727, left), one of the most brilliant scientists of all time (and the discoverer of gravity), spent as much time studying alchemy as "true" science.

SERVANTS OF THE DEVIL

Seventeenth-century Scotland was a fearful place. Close Bible study led to a fascination with the real power of evil and widespread persecution of witches.

In 1649, the witch-finder John Kincaid found the devil's marks on a group of men and women from Dirleton, east of Edinburgh. They confessed to meeting the devil, who appeared as a "greate, blak man."

After their trial the witches were imprisoned in the gloomy vaults of Dirleton Castle (*right*), from where they were taken to execution.

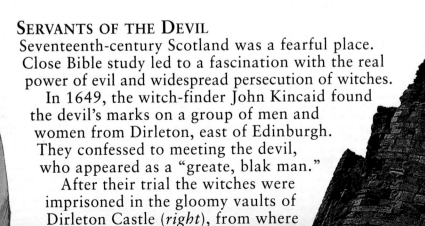

THE SALEM WITCH TRIALS

Salem, Massachusetts, 1692. A group of girls aged between 4 and 20 sit around the fire listening to stories of a female slave, Tituba. Two of the girls become hysterical. Shortly afterward, adults complain that the girls have been bewitched.

Arrests are made (*right*) and a trial is held. Of the 150 people accused, 19 people are hanged, one is crushed to death with stones, and two die in prison. Even dogs are executed for witchcraft!

The trials went on until 1693, when local ministers helped to stop the craze. The executions were the last for witchcraft in North America, and also signaled the end of witch trials in Europe as well.

Tumbling Like Hogs (below) *Young girls from Salem on trial for witchcraft. One of the accused was said to have "tumbled about like a hog." No one is quite sure what went on. Some historians think that a local minister, Samuel Paris, used the beliefs of ignorant farmers to accuse villagers who opposed him.*

PILGRIM FATHERS

The colony of Massachusetts was founded by religious refugees who left England in 1620. Known as the "Pilgrim Fathers" (*below*), many of them possessed a strong puritanical faith. They genuinely believed that the devil might appear at any moment. As an English colony, Massachusetts followed English law, so witchcraft was punishable by death.

Sixteen other witches had already been hanged in the region by 1692.

The Last Witch?

The Swiss woman Anna Goddi, hanged in 1782, was the last person in Europe to be executed for witchcraft.

HOLY MOTION POTION

Evil spirits can be driven from a person or place by exorcism. This is a special religious ceremony that a priest may perform only with a bishop's permission.

In earlier times, people believed evil spirits entered and left people by the body's natural openings. This led to some very odd rituals and experiences! Those possessed by a demon might be given a "holy potion" to drink, made up of oil, herbs, and sherry!

BURN HER!

It seems surprising that someone burned as a witch should become a national heroine, but that is exactly what happened to Joan of Arc (1412-1431).

At the age of thirteen, Joan heard voices telling her to drive the English from France. King Charles VII lent her an army which she led to great victories. Sadly, Joan was captured, sold to the English, and put on trial for heresy and witchcraft. Although she defended herself bravely, she was condemned to life imprisonment and told never again to wear men's clothes.

Then the English tricked her into breaking her word and burned her at the stake in Rouen in 1431. She was only nineteen years old. Five hundred years later she became the patron saint of France.

The Fever Word
The age-old magic charm Abracadabra was used as a cure for illness. It was often set out as an inverted pyramid (below).

As the size of the word diminished, the fever was supposed to fade away.

ABRACADABRA
BRACADABR
RACADAB
ACADA
CAD
A

MYSTIC PROTECTION
Charms, from the Latin word for "a song," are magic words or objects designed to ward off evil. A charm worn on the body is an amulet. Popular Christian amulets include crosses and images of St. Christopher. Muslims carry tiny plaques inscribed with verses from the Koran.

The Witches' Gate
Many English churches have a gate at their boundary wall – this was originally designed to keep witches at bay (right).

BOTTLED OUT
In popular superstition, there were few better ways of defeating witchcraft than a "witch bottle" charm (*right*). Those fearing a witch filled the bottle with their urine, some hair, nail clippings, and any sharp objects, such as nails or thorns.

The bottle was then tightly corked and boiled at midnight. This tormented the witch. If the bottle burst, the witch died. But if the cork flew out, she escaped!

Legend has it that Cunning Murrell, the famous English wizard, died from a witch bottle filled from a bewitched donkey!

The Living Heart
The English burned the teenage Joan of Arc (right) for witchcraft. One record tells how she reduced onlookers to tears with her incredible bravery.

Her heart was found among the ashes and thrown into the Seine River.

FATAL MARKS

Any unusual blemish – scar, mole, or wart – might be a "devil's mark" and a sure sign of witchcraft. Witch-hunters publicly stripped suspects naked to search for such marks. They also stuck sharp probes into the skin, seeking an area (an invisible devil's mark) where the suspect did not bleed or feel pain.

The Power of Rumor

English queen Anne Boleyn (right), was almost accused of witchcraft by her husband Henry VIII. She had a tiny sixth finger and was rumored to possess a third nipple for feeding her familiar spirits! In the end, Henry had her beheaded as a traitor.

Rue

Vervain

Dill

PROTECTIVE PLANTS

There is an old rhyme that says

Rue, vervain, and dill
Hinder witches from their will

Rowan berries

Many other plants were supposed to guard against witchcraft. Celts thought the red-berried rowan, or "witch tree," was best. A cross woven from rowan was sometimes tied to a cow's tail with scarlet thread!

31

WITCH DOCTORS AND ZOMBIES

African magic was divided into witchcraft and sorcery. Witches were generally women that inherited their magical powers. They were said to harm people with words and thoughts alone, and met at night around a fire, even indulging in cannibalism. Their familiars were hyenas, owls, baboons, and dwarfs.

Unlike the witches of Europe, they served several evil spirits rather than a single devil; but like them, they were usually scapegoats whose wicked work explained misfortunes that did not have obvious natural causes.

Sorcery could be learned by anyone, and involved potions and complicated magic spells.

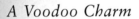

A Voodoo Charm

VOODOO

When millions of African slaves were shipped to the New World in the 18th century, they brought with them their tribal religions. These become *candomblé* in Brazil, *obeayisne* in Jamaica, and *voodoo* in the Caribbean island of Haiti.

Voodoo means "spirit" in the Fon language of West Africa. Believers worship spirits like Zoka, the god of farming, and Baron Samedi, lord of the dead. Voodoo ceremonies are highly elaborate and involve dancing and singing, which is thought to please the gods.

MAGIC MEDICINE

The traditional healer in many African societies is the witch doctor (*above*). Usually a man, he treats all forms of illness, from headaches to wounds, with a mixture of magic and herbal remedies. People used to ridicule witch doctors' powers. They now recognize that many of their cures have a sound scientific foundation.

Trial By Chicken (main picture)
The Azande people of West Africa feed poison to chickens and mention the name of someone suspected of witchcraft. If the creature dies, the suspect is guilty!

A vévé, or symbolic pattern, has been drawn on the floor with flour to create a place for spirits to appear.

Spirits and witches. Writers have long been fascinated by the traditional magic of Africa. British writer Rider Haggard's adventure *King Solomon's Mines* (filmed in 1975, *above*) features Gagool, an old wicked witch who is the only person who knows the secret of the mines.

More recently, in *The Famished Road*, Nigerian writer Ben Okri features in his story a tormented "spirit child" who moves between the human and spirit worlds.

The Living Dead. Zombies, corpses revived by magic and put to work by priests (*oungan*), are the most terrifying Voodoo legend. Robotlike and without intelligence, they have gruesome powers. Michael Jackson played one in his video *Thriller* (*above*). Scientists think such trances may in fact be caused by drugs, like those in the spines of poisonous fish (*right*).

SHAMANS AND SPIRITS

If Iroquois children misbehaved, Long Nose the evil spirit might carry them off in a basket and devour them. To the Iroquois, like other Native American tribes, magic was part of religion. A mystical force, known as *orenda* (the Iroquois word for "Great Spirit") controlled the world.

Good and bad lesser spirits, such as Long Nose, linked humans to the Great Spirit.

Part of a religion stretching back to the Stone Age (*left*), the shaman, or medicine man, had the power to protect people from the bad luck the spirits might bring.

Spirit Levelers (below) – *a rattle for summoning animal spirits, and a charm for luring the souls of fish into Inuit traps.*

Bird Rattle

Soapstone fish charm

THE POWER OF THE ANGAKUK

Magic played a vital part in the lives of the Inuit people of the frozen north. Surrounded by danger and darkness, they relied on the magic charms of their *angakuk* (a male or female wizard) to guard them against all perils.

One *angakuk* is said to have grown walrus tusks to defend himself. Another was buried for three days in a frozen lake, but emerged completely unharmed!

Ghost Dancers
During the final destruction of Native American cultures by European settlers, a prophet named Wovoka declared that all those performing the Ghost Dance (left) would be protected from harm. Black Elk, a Sioux, wore a ghost shirt as he danced (right) at Wounded Knee Creek in 1890. He was still wounded – but 350 others died in the massacre.

Sucking Out Evil
Holding magic charms, an Inuit medicine man performs a ritual dance to cure a sick girl. The shaman "sucks out" of the patient's body any evil spirits causing an illness.

POLE POWER

A totem is a sacred object that both represents and protects a person or tribe. The word comes from the language of the Algonquin Indians and means "my guardian spirit."

Totems can be plants, animals, or objects. Totem poles, found on the Pacific coast of North America, are tall tree trunks carved or painted with totems (*left*).

Shield (above) *painted with magical signs to protect the owner.*

MEDICINE MEN. Among the Ojibwa tribe of Canada, everyone has some of the shaman's powers, but some members are more powerful than others. The *jossakid* are responsible for "the shaking tent," a ceremony where the veiled shaman does battle with spirits, while *wabeno* are known for their fire magic.

STRAIGHT TO THE HEART

In the 14th and 15th centuries, the Aztecs created a highly developed empire in what is now Mexico. But religion still dominated their way of life.

The Aztecs believed that human sacrifice was essential to the harmony of the cosmos, and that they had a special duty to feed the gods human blood. If they failed, the sun would not rise, and the universe would end.

Aztec sacrifices sometimes involved cutting the beating hearts from live human beings (right).

A DEMON QUEEN?

King Solomon was worried. He was expecting a visit from the beautiful Queen of Sheba, and had heard her mother was a dangerous *jinn*, or demon.

As jinns had hairy legs, Solomon needed to get a glimpse of the queen's calves as soon as possible. So he arranged for a mirror to be laid on the floor to look like water. When his guest saw it, she lifted her skirts so they would not get wet. To his relief, Solomon saw that her legs were as smooth as marble.

Sheba's visit was a success, and Solomon fell in love with her. In another legend, he is said to have conquered the jinns with a ring inscribed with God's name.

The Evil Eye
The ancient and widespread belief in the Evil Eye (top) stems from the idea that the glance of certain people can bring disaster.

One Moroccan proverb says "The Evil Eye owns two-thirds of the grave-yard," and as late as 1948, a German man was taken to court for casting the Evil Eye on his neighbors' cattle!

YOU ARE MY LUCKY STAR?
Astronomy (*above*) began in the ancient worlds of Greece, Rome, China, and India. In the 8th and 9th centuries it was taken up by Muslim scholars.

Men such as Abu Ma'shar gave it new complexity and subtlety. But priests did not like the idea that stars, not God, ruled men's lives, and the study was suppressed.

Calf Love (above)
The queen of Sheba greets King Solomon. Until he saw her smooth legs in the mirror, the king thought she might be a demon.

FIERY SPIRITS

Muslims believed in the existence of Jinns, spirits that lived in the mountains surrounding the world.

Although they were sometimes thought of as the servants of God (just like angels), they were tricky characters. They were made of fire but could be tamed with the magic words, *Azamtu atalkum*, "I command you!"

Jinn sometimes disguised themselves as animals such as scorpions or insects.

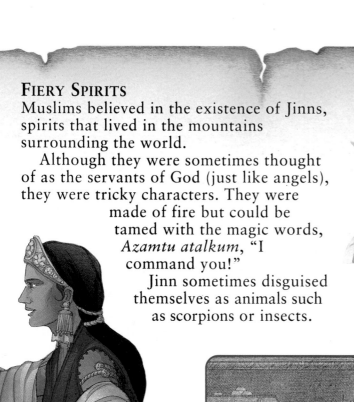

G IVE IT A GOOD RUB! The oriental tale of Aladdin tells of a boy's struggle with a wicked magician. When the magic lamp is rubbed, a genie appears and grants Aladdin three wishes (*left*). The genie builds Aladdin a wonderful palace, but the magician transports it to Africa after tricking Aladdin's wife into giving him the lamp.

In the end, Aladdin regains the lamp and flies the palace back to China.

ISLAM AND MAGIC

Unlike Christianity, Islam accepts magic as one of the legitimate "occult sciences."

Sixty-six verses in the Koran mention magic, which is seen as part of God's knowledge shown to humankind by the fallen angels.

Don't Wiggle!
A modern Islamic exorcist attempts to expel a Jinn by taping the victim's toes together (right).

THE MASKHARA DERVISHES

This Arab tribe, once dedicated to a horned god, performed wild dances, their faces blackened by a cosmetic – giving us the word "mascara!"

DIPPER POWER

Magic and sorcery run deep in Oriental culture. The Buddha magically crossed the Ganges just before he died. The Chinese *wu* and Japanese *miko* are sorcerers with power to mediate between the human and spirit worlds.

In 23 A.D., the Chinese emperor Wang Mang was in trouble. His country was in turmoil and his enemies were increasing.

Desperate for help, Wang asked the mighty god of the Big Dipper (also known as the Plow) constellation for help. Wang got in touch with the god by using a metal instrument designed to work out the constellation's position (*main picture*).

Did the god dislike the emperor? Or did Wang use the instrument wrongly? Whatever the reason, soon after, he was overthrown in the Revolt of the Red Eyebrows!

Deadly Drafts
Even today, "good winds" (feng sui) are considered vitally important to Chinese people across the world.

New buildings are designed according to spiritual rules so that "good" air can pass through them. Mirrors (top) are also used to ward off evil spirits.

Not Just a Bunch of Old Herbs

In recent years there has been a growing recognition in the West of the healing powers of ancient Chinese herbal medicine (left) and acupuncture (treating disease by sticking needles into special places in the body).

SUN'S RECIPES
Alchemy probably began in China. As early as the 5th century B.C., Chinese doctors were seeking a potion to give eternal life. This "elixir of life" was thought to be made of liquid gold, a metal that never tarnishes.

Sun Ssu-miao wrote the most famous Chinese work on alchemy, *Great Secrets of Alchemy*, in the 7th century A.D. Its several magic recipes contain mercury, sulfur, and the poison arsenic. If Sun's elixirs did not bring eternal life, they would certainly have brought a stomachache!

CHINESE MYTHOLOGY is full of stories of good and bad magicians and humans battling against the spirit world.
An evil sorcerer (*left*) terrifies the inhabitants of San Francisco's Chinatown in the 1989 comedy *Big Trouble in Little China*.

THE TERRIBLE CANNIBAL

In Russian legend the witch Baba-Yaga haunts the countryside. The tall and skinny old hag has a long sharp nose and teeth, and breasts of iron (*right*)!

She flies on a flaming mortar, sweeping as she goes. Her house is protected with a wall of bones, the remains of the victims of her cannibalistic feasts.

NOT SO MAGICAL MAO!

When the Communists came to power in China in 1949, they tried to put an end to traditional beliefs in myth and magic. However, in later life, Mao Zedong, the Communist leader, relied on the myth of his own superhuman abilities to maintain control.

At the age of seventy he was filmed swimming 60 miles up the Yangtze River. In fact he had swum nothing like this distance and was supported by scuba divers under the water!

The Psychic Detectives of India
Part of an ancient tradition of magic, in 1909 three psychics helped the Indian police track down the murderer of a French official (right). Mediums have also been used by police forces in Europe.

AROUND THE CAULDRON

"This Devil presides at their Sabbats, when they all kiss him and dance around him. Then he envelopes them in total darkness, and they all... give themselves up to the grossest and most disgusting debauchery." So wrote Pope Gregory IX to the priests near Bremen in Germany, warning them of covens of witches in their region.

The letter mentions many supposed features of a Sabbat: The presence of the devil, the dancing and strange rituals, and the feasting and immoral behavior. Though most evidence for Sabbats comes from 16th century trials (where torture was used to produce confessions), similar images are used today by churchmen concerned at Satanic practices.

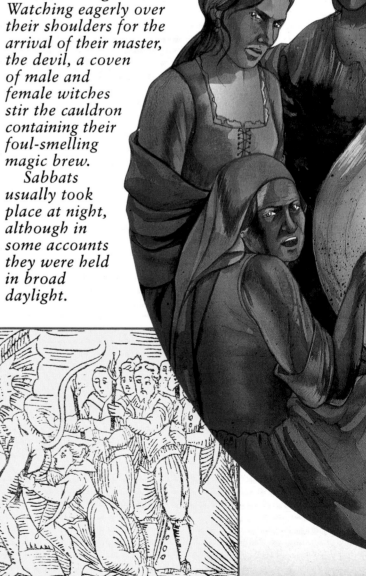

LORD OF THE RINGS. Sorcery is concerned with the eternal struggle between good and evil. This is the theme of J.R.R. Tolkien's immensely popular *Lord of the Rings* series of novels, full of magic and mystery (and made into a cartoon, *above*).

Brewer's Delight
Watching eagerly over their shoulders for the arrival of their master, the devil, a coven of male and female witches stir the cauldron containing their foul-smelling magic brew.
Sabbats usually took place at night, although in some accounts they were held in broad daylight.

THE DEVIL'S DANCE
In the Middle Ages dancing was common in Christian churches. Not surprisingly, witches were said to have devised special dances for their own "services."

The music was played on a simple pipe and drum, but the dancing itself was often frenzied. Some witches danced naked, others dressed in men's clothes. In Francesco Guazzo's fantastical *Compendium of Witches* (1608), they are even shown kissing the Devil's backside (*right*)!

BUBBLE TROUBLE

There was supposedly plenty of food and drink at a Sabbat, and the witches often got drunk. Their hell-brew was made in a cauldron or the skull of a recently beheaded human! A cock's intestines and other nasty ingredients only made the drinker feel sick (*above*, in clockwise order – mistletoe, mandrake root, snake, toad, and deadly nightshade). But carefully chosen herbs might make them even drunker.

Flying High

Witches often confessed to flying to Sabbats. There is some scientific evidence for this mistaken belief. Before takeoff witches rubbed their bodies with magical ointment. Some ingredients, like bat's blood, were useless, others contained powerful herbal drugs like belladonna (deadly nightshade). When the drug entered the bloodstream, it gave the witch a high and led her to believe she really could fly!

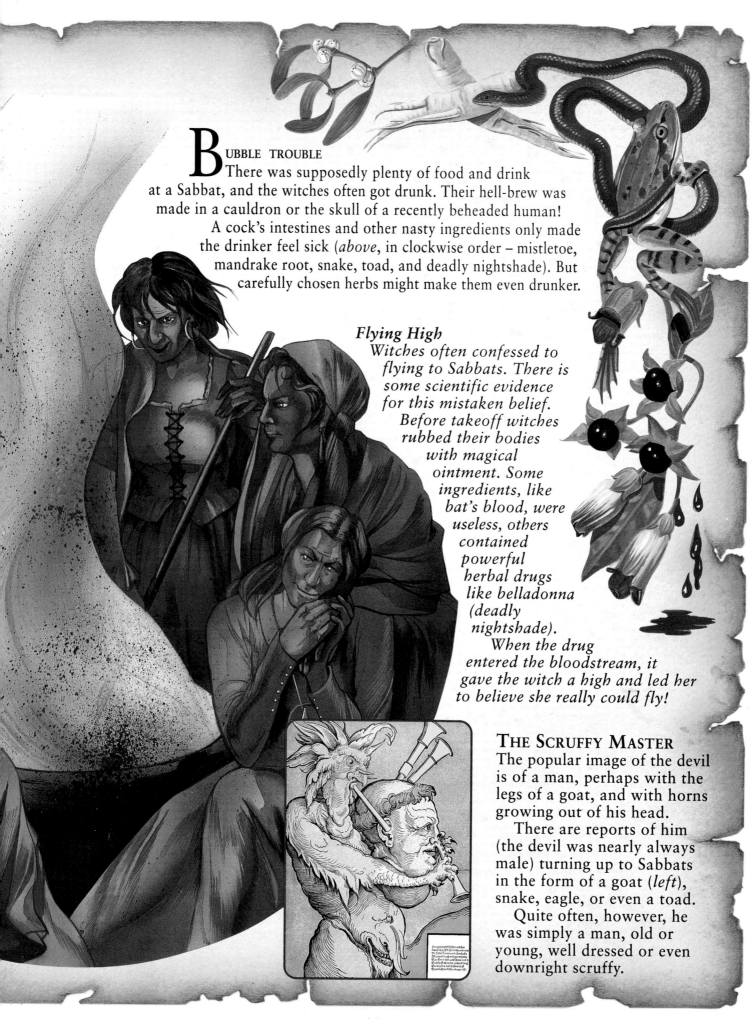

THE SCRUFFY MASTER

The popular image of the devil is of a man, perhaps with the legs of a goat, and with horns growing out of his head.

There are reports of him (the devil was nearly always male) turning up to Sabbats in the form of a goat (*left*), snake, eagle, or even a toad.

Quite often, however, he was simply a man, old or young, well dressed or even downright scruffy.

THE RISE OF REASON

About one hundred years ago, a group of Italian gold-hunters cruelly sacrificed a young boy. They believed his blood would bring them luck. German rural communities still practiced pagan rites in the 1920s.

However, stories like this are now very rare, at least in Europe. There are several reasons for the decline in belief in magic. Religion has less hold over people and scientific research has disproved many of the magical superstitions associated with sorcery. Populations are better educated and fewer live in remote rural communities buzzing with malicious rumor and gossip.

The Magus
This elaborate book used for calling up spirits, or grimoire, was written by Francis Barrett in 1801. The page below shows Cassiel, the angel who rules Saturday.

THE BEAUTIFUL WITCH. The poet Percy Bysshe Shelley (1792-1822) was expelled from Oxford University for defending atheism. Many young people educated in the Age of Reason found the traditional Christian teaching unacceptable. Belief in the devil declined with belief in God.

In his poem *The Witch of Atlas*, Shelley reversed some of the ancient superstitions. His witch was a beautiful young woman who used her magic for good rather than evil purposes. She sees into men's souls and then foils their evil plans.

TESTAMENT OF MAGIC

Today magicians are generally entertainers, not weavers of wicked spells. We are amazed at their skill, but we do not fear them for their magical powers.

The 19th-century magician Eliphas Lévi, however, believed that strongly that God was responsible for good and evil (*right*) and used traditional practices from the Cabbala, a body of mystical thought from the Jewish religion.

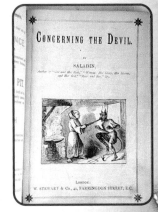

This is concerned with the relationship between letters and numbers. Passages of text may be written upside down, and letters are added up to form significant numbers.

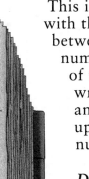

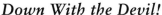

Down With the Devil!
"There is enough in Hell to keep a visitor interested for a long time, especially if he have some taste for chemistry." Thus mocked the unbeliever W. Stewart Ross in his pamphlet Concerning the Devil (right).
Ross and several other Victorians devoted their lives to attacking religion, largely for the harm they believed it had done. They had no time for God or His enemy the devil.

A SCHOOL FOR SORCERY
The 19th-century magician Francis Barrett, an authority on magic amulets and talismans, offered to open a school for magic – but only 12 students came forward!

SABBATS OF FUN

By the 18th century, serious belief in witches and devil worship was all but dead in England. That did not stop the well-known aristocrat Sir Francis Dashwood (*above right*) from putting ancient traditions to a new purpose.

Dashwood formed a secret society, known as the "Knights of St. Francis of Wycombe" or the "Hell Fire Club."

The club's meetings were like a Sabbat, but without the devil. Many of the rich and famous attended the parties in the club's caves (*far left*), hell-bent on pleasure in all its forms!

WITCHES NEVER DIE

Wherever we look there are still witches. They appear as figures of fun in films. Many children's books feature witches and magic. They are popular TV characters and crop up in countless gruesome horror movies.

Superstition is still taken seriously. Millions dread Friday the 13th and will not walk under ladders. Horoscopes in popular newspapers are widely read. A few people openly admit to being witches. Witch doctors practice widely in Africa and witch societies are widespread. Members believe in the power of magic, but they are "white witches," working for good.

Finally, there are a few adults who still believe in the powers of darkness. Witches, it seems, have discovered the secret of eternal life at last – they never die!

Satanic kolduns (right) *claim to work through the devil. But the real power of these modern witches comes from the beliefs of ordinary Russians, thirsting for miracles in a time of dramatic change and great hardship.*

A THING OF THE PAST?
After the collapse of Communism, *kolduns*, or witches, returned with a vengeance to everyday Russian life. Wizards even appear on television and have more in common with wealthy American evangelists than traditional devil-worshipers.

Kolduns claim to use white magic to perform tasks from finding stolen cars to arranging love matches. Some charge their customers thousands of dollars, but the traditional witches, the *babushkas,* work for bags of food from poor clients.

REDS UNDER THE BED
Though witchcraft is no longer a crime in many countries, the witch hunt lives on. After World War II, the United States and the Soviet Union lived in fear of each other.

Some Americans, led by Senator Joseph McCarthy, genuinely believed that communists (nicknamed "Reds") were secretly working to take over the country. Thousands were unfairly condemned until the scare died down and McCarthy was discredited.

THE WIZARD OF OZ. Witches remain a popular subject in both children's and adult films. Perhaps the most famous film witch is the Wicked Witch of the West, from the 1939 classic *The Wizard of Oz* (above). The wizard of the title, however, turns out to be a fraud!

The Druids
Little is known about the Druids of pre-Roman Europe, but it seems they held the same festival days as witches. Today's druids (left) see druidism as a way of life, rather than as a religion.

SATANISM
In a few dark corners of the Earth old-fashioned devil-worship is still practiced. It generally goes by the name of Satanism and its rites are closely guarded. Most modern witches want nothing to do with it.

Every now and again, however, Satanists get into the news, usually when they have committed a crime.

LITTLE DEVILS Parents have scared their children into good behavior with images of the devil for centuries.

This one (*left*) comes from a pamphlet written in 1721, titled *A Timely Warning to Rash and Disobedient Children!*

Today's Witches
Quite how many witches there are in the West today, no one knows, but since the repeal of laws outlawing witchcraft, there has certainly been a growing interest in magic.

Most of today's witches use spells, ceremonies and herbal formulas to work good magic (main picture).

MODERN MEDICINE MEN
In the 1990s there is a growing interest in the healing link between mind and body. Non-western religions such as those of the Native Americans and those in Africa are no longer regarded as primitive devil-worshiping superstitions.

Indeed, medicine men like Rolling Thunder (*above left*) are now being asked to show their healing skills to doctors.

BEWITCHED! The best loved TV witch was the housewife Samantha (*left*), from the popular American comedy series *Bewitched*.
Unknown to everyone else, Sam and her witch daughter Tabitha (a traditional name for a witch's familiar cat) use their powers to take life easy. Sam has only to twitch her nose and the housework is done – by magic!

WITCH WORDS

Alchemy The search for a substance that brings eternal life and also for the means of turning base metals into gold. Alchemists used special symbols (*left*) for their chemicals.

Amulet Small container for a magic charm, to ward off evil.

Astrology Belief that lives and personalities are influenced by the planets and stars.

Cathars Members of a medieval heretical sect, widespread in southern France and northern Spain, who believed that God was a source of evil as well as of good. Also known as *Albigensians*.

Cauldron Large cooking pot often used by witches for making their magic brew.

Charm Words or an object supposed to protect from spells.

Devil's marks Marks on the body, such as scars or warts, that have been put there by the devil to identify his followers.

Divination Fortune-telling; telling the future.

Druids Celtic sorcerers. Modern druids perform pagan rituals rather than magic.

Elixir of life Substance giving eternal life.

Evil eye Casting a spell on someone by looking at them (its symbol is *center*).

Familiar Creature, such as a cat or baboon, that helps a witch.

Feng sui Chinese belief in winds that bring good and bad fortune.

Glamor The power to change shape.

Grimoire A spell book (*left*).

Halloween All Hallows Eve, the day before All Saints' Day.

Heretic Unbeliever in true faith.

Horoscope Chart of astrological predictions.

Host Communion bread.

Inquisition Catholic Church's investigation for rooting out heresy.

Jinn Muslim spirit made from fire.

Metamorphosis Transforming from one type of body to another; for example, a witch might metamorphose into a cat.

Numerology Fortune-telling by using significant numbers.

Ouija board Board marked with letters of the alphabet. Used to receive messages from the other world.

Palmistry Fortune-telling by the study of hands.

Papal bull Official announcement by the pope.

Protestantism Religion of those who broke away from the Roman Catholic Church in the 16th century.

Ritual Formal religious or magical practice.

Roman Catholicism Christian church headed by the pope.

Rosicrucians Mystical 17th-century Christian sect.

Rune Ancient Germanic letter of writing.

Sabbat Gathering of witches.

Satanism Modern-day devil worship.

Sorcerer Male performer of magic; a wizard.

Spell Words or movements that make magic happen.

Tarot Cards Cards for telling the future.

Totem Object adopted to represent a person or group.

Voodoo Magical religion based in the Caribbean and the southern U.S. Belief in gods and spirits.

Wizard A male version of a witch, sometimes called a warlock.

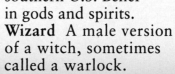

WITCHES' TIMELINE

50,000 B.C. First evidence of magic – early peoples buried bears as part of their rituals.

30,000 B.C. First talismans in use as protection against spirits. At about the same time, shamans (*left*) were probably the first magic makers.

5,000–2,000 B.C. Ancient Egypt, birthplace of Western magic.

c.2,500 B.C. The Celts raise great standing stones, e.g. at Stonehenge, England.

5th century B.C. Alchemy probably begins in ancient China.

A.D. 2nd century *The Golden Ass* is written by Lucius Apuleius.

100–800 A.D. Christian missionaries convert pagan Europe.

1135 Geoffrey of Monmouth writes the *History of the Kings of Britain* and creates the mythical character of Merlin (*center*).

1208 Pope Innocent III condemns the Cathars and begins a campaign to wipe them out.

1229 The Inquisition is founded to lead the attack on witchcraft as the Church begins to view witches not just as pagans but as allies of the devil.

11th–13th centuries Crusaders in the Middle East come into contact with the eastern tradition of magic.

13th century Golden age of alchemy (*below*), although it continued until the arrival of modern science in the 19th century.

1431 Joan of Arc burned as a witch by the English, at Rouen in France.

1484 Pope Innocent VIII's papal bull supports witch-hunters Kraemer and Sprenger, and begins the witch craze. In the next 200 years, over 300,000 witches are executed in Europe.

1555 Nostradamus writes *Centuries*, his series of predictions.

1584 Reginald Scot writes the *Discoverie of Witchcraft*, arguing that witchcraft does not really exist.

16th–19th centuries The transportation of black slaves from Africa to New World brings the voodoo religion to America.

1606 William Shakespeare's *Macbeth,* with its three witches, is first performed.

1608 Death of John Dee, who claimed to have found the secret of eternal life!

1614 The Rosicrucian movement is founded in Germany.

1647 Death of Matthew Hopkins, "Witch-Finder General" (*top*).

1692 Salem witch trials result in 19 executions but signal the end of witch hunts in America and Europe.

1750–1762 The heyday of Francis Dashwood and the Hell Fire Club.

1782 Anna Goddi hanged, the last person to be executed for witchcraft in Europe.

1801 Francis Barrett writes his grimoire *The Magus.*

1820 English poet Percy Bysshe Shelley writes *The Witch of Atlas*.

1890 350 Sioux Indians are killed by U.S. troops at Wounded Knee as they perform the Ghost Dance.

20th century Witchcraft laws are repealed across Europe, leading to growth in groups like Druids (*right*).

1976 World Health Organization recommends that witch doctors should join African medical teams.

INDEX

Photo credits *Abbreviations: t – top, m – middle, b – bottom, l – left, r – right.*
Cover, 4-5, 6, 11l, 16t & m, 18t, 19, 23t, 25t & b, 26t, 28, 29tl, 30t & m, 36, 37m, 39, 40b & 42m – Mary Evans Picture Library; 6-7 & 17 – Warner Brothers (courtesy Kobal); 7t & b, 22, 23b, 26b, 35, 44-45m & 45tr & br – Fortean Picture Library; 8, 13tl, 20tl & b, 30b & 38b – Roger Vlitos; 9 – Ancient Art & Architecture Collection; 10t – Bruce Coleman Collection; 10b, 14t, 18m, 20tr & m, 21, 40t & 41 – AKG London; 11tr & 44bl – Ronald Grant Archive; 13tr, 14m, 27b & 42m – Stewart Ross; 13b – Orion/Warner Brothers (courtesy Kobal); 15 & 31– Hulton Deutsch Collection; 29tr, 32, 37b, 38m, 44bl, 44-45t & 47br – Frank Spooner Pictures; 33t – Cannon Films (courtesy Kobal); 33b – Rex Features; 38b – 20th Century films (courtesy Kobal); 40m – Saul Zaentz Productions (courtesy Kobal); 44-45 – Columbia Pictures (courtesy Kobal).